How to Get Out of Credit Card Debt

How to Save Money and Fix Your Credit (2 Manuscripts in 1 Book)

By David A. Hunter

I0390379

HOW TO SAVE MONEY
Save Your Money, Even as A Teenager

By DAVID A. HUNTER

Disclaimer

The views expressed within this book are those of the author alone. The information contained within this book is based on the opinions, experiences, and observations of the author and should not be used to replace the advice of a competent professional. The information contained within this book is not legal, financial, investment, or any other kind of professional advice. Neither the author nor publisher will assume liability or responsibility for any loss or damage related directly or indirectly to the information contained within this book. Neither the author nor publisher are engaged in rendering professional services.

The author has attempted to be as accurate as possible with the information contained within this book. Neither the author nor publisher will assume liability or responsibility for any errors, omissions, or inconsistencies.

Table of Contents

Why Should You Save Money When You Are So Young?

Personally, I found it easier to save money when I had a specific goal in mind, but it can be challenging to save money simply for the sake of saving money.

It takes the right kind of motivation to accomplish your goals in life, and saving money requires just as much motivation as the rest of your goals.

Be wise and realize that the amount of effort you put into something now will reflect what you get out of it later.

I remember saving money for my first car when I was only 14 years old. I was laughed at because I wasn't even old enough to drive at the time, but I knew about the importance of planning in advance.

Certain people might give you a rough time because they only see a tiny fraction of the picture.

The picture begins to expand as you start making progress towards achieving your goals.

You will begin to gain reassurance.

You will realize that you did the right thing.

There were also times when I would get discouraged. I remember making such little money at my job, I started to ask, "What's the point?"

At the time, I didn't think I should bother saving money since I was making so little of it. I figured that it would take me the rest of my life at that rate to save enough money to buy anything that was worth having.

Due to this negative mindset, I started wasting my money on all kinds of different things that I didn't need. I thought that making a lot of money was the only way to have a good amount of money in your bank account, so I basically gave up. It took me years to finally realize what a big mistake I was making by thinking that way.

I look back now and realize that there is no excuse to not save your money, even as a teenager.

Making money is only one part of the game.

You should dedicate just as much time and effort into saving your money as you dedicate to making money.

Think of making money as drinking water and saving money as food. You really need both in order to survive. How much you need will depend on the person and what their plans are, but everyone needs at least a little of both.

It can be difficult to see the importance of saving money when you are really young; just like it can be difficult to see the importance of drinking water when you are only 6 years old. If I felt thirsty when I was 6 years old, I would just go ahead and drink flavored drinks with sugar in them. It took me years before I decided that I should really be drinking water more often. Buying the wrong things instead of saving your money is like drinking things that actually end up dehydrating you. It just doesn't make sense in the long run.

It's easy enough to understand the desire for making and spending money, but we seem to get lost and confused when it comes to saving it.

Many people would panic if they stopped making money, but they seem to be perfectly carefree with the idea of not saving it. Sometimes we have to learn the hard way.

Some of us might not see the importance of saving money until the flow of cash stops.

Don't make that mistake.

Don't wait until something dramatic happens before you finally open your eyes to the importance of saving money.

You need to have just as much respect for saving money as you do for making money.

Don't be negative about saving money.

Have a positive outlook on your life and see each dollar that you save as another step closer to reaching your goals, even if you don't have any financial goals as of right now.

There are so many different reasons to save money, and you never know what you might need the extra cash for in the future.

It's always good to save more than what you think you will need.

For instance, let's say that you get a job and then you plan to buy a car. The car that you want costs $12,000.

You finally manage to save $12,000, so you go ahead and buy the car. You do the math and figure that your job will give you just enough money to cover the gasoline costs and insurance bills. A few months go by and you're doing well, keeping up with all of your gasoline and insurance payments. One day your car doesn't start.

You read the owner's manual, but your still not sure how to fix the problem. You're not even really sure what's wrong. You end up calling a tow truck to take it to the car shop. You find out that your battery is dead and it needs to be replaced.

The entire cost including the tow truck, labor, and the battery totals in at around $200.

Now you might be in a mess because you only considered the costs of gasoline and insurance when you bought the car.

You don't have to think about every single thing that could happen when you buy something like a car, but you do need to consider the very real possibility that you might end up needing more money than you initially thought.

It's nearly impossible to think about all of the possible reasons for needing extra money in the future, but it seems that there is always something.

Things To Consider Before You Buy Something Expensive

We often get so caught up with the things that we want in life, we can easily fail to realize all of the additional costs that come along with them.

We have the ambition to go after the things that we want in life, but we tend to look right past the burden of responsibility that we will have to carry.

I was aware that there would be a monthly bill from the internet service provider when I bought my laptop computer, but I didn't think about the battery that would need to be replaced after a couple of years. My laptop was already expensive enough, but if I would have thought about the battery, I would have made much more of an effort to keep it charged.

Even a cheaper purchase can turn into something expensive fast.

Here are some examples:

-A BLU-RAY player can tempt you to spend hundreds of dollars on BLU-RAY discs

-A video game console can tempt you to buy more and more video games

-A cheap car could end up costing a lot of money in repairs

-Cheap batteries might cost a few dollars less, but they usually don't last half as long as the better ones

-Free tickets to a baseball game could end up costing you $10 for parking and $20 for food and drinks

-Getting a job that's simply too far away might end up costing you a lot of money in gasoline

- "Free" checking accounts could have fees attached to them that can start adding up

That's just a short list to get you to start thinking about the other side of the story. That doesn't mean you shouldn't ever buy or do any of these things.

You just want to start thinking about the costs that you don't always see right away. I know what it's like to get excited about something and only focus on the positive things about whatever it is that you wish to buy.

You don't have to be a pessimist and say, "There is no point in ever doing anything because everything is always a waste of money."

Prepare yourself by taking the time to weigh out the pros and cons of your purchase before you make the transaction.

Here are some questions to ask yourself:

-Do I really need this?

-Am I still going to want this a few years from now?

-Will it depreciate fast?

-Will I be able to sell it after I no longer have any use for it?

-Is this a good investment?

-Does this bring me any closer to my goals?

-Will I look back one day and regret not buying this?

Another mistake I made when I was growing up was investing in basketball cards.

Everyone kept telling me about how much money they were going to be worth one day, so I kept collecting them. I learned that having something of value and getting people to pay you for it are two different things.

You could buy something for $700, keep it in excellent condition, and have somebody offer you just $125 for it. I would have been much better off simply saving my money instead of trying to invest it in material objects that only have a possibility of bringing you more money.

Another drawback to buying things that you hope to sell is that you have to be very careful that you are not selling the wrong things. Many things out there are illegal to resell, so it's really not worth it.

It's usually better to save your money unless they provide immediate value. A basketball card doesn't really provide you with immediate value. It simply sits there while you wait for it to hopefully make you some money one day.

A book can provide immediate value because the words inside of it can become absorbed by your brain as soon as you read it.

Your mind can gather and process the information right away. A movie can provide immediate value because it can entertain you as soon as you start watching it.

Music provides value as soon as you start listening to it. You don't have to wait for your favorite song to become popular before you start enjoying it.

Don't buy things that just sit there just because you believe there might be a slight chance that they'll make you money one of these days.

Are These Things Really What You Want?

Whether you realize it or not, many people that you interact with can actually make up your mind for you when it comes to how you should spend your money.

There are commercials, previews, and many other things that might cause you to buy something that you never would have wanted in the first place.

When you watch a movie with a boring story-line, the music can actually pull you in if you like the sound of it.

There can also be special effects added to many of the scenes.

When it comes to life in general, you need to learn how to filter through all of the "special effects" that you might happen to see or hear.

Are you buying something just because it looks cool? Are you doing something just because everyone else seems to be doing it?

You have to get to the core of whatever it is that you wish to spend your money on.

Picture what it would look like without all of that fancy stuff attached to it. The best things in life will not always be wrapped up in an expensive looking package. As they say, "Big things come in small packages."

Look for things that provide something that you can use now and later on in the future.

Most people regret buying things that don't end up lasting very long.

There are plenty of things out there to buy that can be a lot of fun, but it makes more sense to stick with things that will actually provide value for years to come.

Here are some examples of things that only provide short-lasting value:

-Fireworks

-Coffee

-Junk Food

-Renting Movies

-Amusement Parks

-Going on "Shopping Sprees"

These types of things are known to give you a "quick thrill," but then you feel empty all over again.

Having a small collection of used DVDS or BLU-RAY discs that you own can be better than spending money every single week on renting movies.

I've always had a collection of movies that I rotate my way through as the year goes on. I will basically cycle through the same movies year after year.

As long as you don't watch the same movie again too soon, it shouldn't feel too repetitious. I'll watch the Christmas movies around December, movies with summer themes in the summer, and so on. I usually watch every movie in my collection about once a year.

I always thought of renting movies as the worst of both worlds. At least going to the movie theater can be entertaining. As for owning a movie, you can watch it again and again whenever you get the urge to do so. I still can't see any real benefits to renting movies though.

You pay for it, watch it on a T.V. screen, and then you have to hurry to bring it right back before you get charged with a late fee. They usually give teenagers a rough time when you try to rent movies anyway.

Coffee can give you a "caffeine boost" for a little while, but you will just end up wanting another one after it wears off. I used to drink a lot of that stuff, but once I stopped, I started to wonder why I ever drank it to begin with.

The trouble with "shopping sprees" is that people usually buy too many things that they won't find as interesting a few weeks later as when they initially bought them.

Start weeding out the things that simply fade away too fast. Focus on the things that will actually be worth spending your money on in the long-term.

Here are some things that will provide value for a longer period of time:

-Clothes

-Jewelry

-Books that you own

-A Stereo

-Movies that you own

-A Pool Table

-A Dart Board

-Board Games

These types of things usually just require a one time fee, and then you can continue to reap the benefits for years to come.

These things can be fun to buy, fun to have, and they'll also provide you with a longer-lasting type of satisfaction.

Obviously, jewelry can be very expensive, but at least it's worth more than junk food or a cup of coffee.

You can have jewelry for years, and it will still hold some kind of value. It's a different story with a cup of coffee.

It's better to put your money towards things that you will still find interesting and entertaining time after time.

It's like the difference between having many seeds or just one single plant. If you buy just one plant, there is a good chance that it will just wither away sooner or later. If you buy a package of seeds, you can plant another one after the other plant dies.

Start picturing each purchase you make as a future investment. Decide whether or not it will be something that you can still benefit from later on.

Books give you information that you can use for years to come, and a pool table can bring you entertainment for years to come.

Chances are that you will not be looking back many years later actually regretting that you didn't spend more money on junk food.

You would be much more likely to look back and regret that you did not invest your time and money into things that were more worthwhile.

Can You Still Go Out With Your Friends And Have A Good Time?

Unless you're trying to get rid of your friends, it's usually not a good idea to avoid hanging out with them.

To begin or maintain a friendship, it takes more than just talking to each other on the phone. Your friends are going to want to go out and do something.

Often enough, many of those things that your friends want to do are going to involve spending some money.

You need to find a way to balance everything out. You don't want to reject your friends, but you don't want to waste your money either.

You can't keep saying "No" to your friends when they ask you to come with them to do something.

What you can do is make an effort to maximize the amount of time that you spend with your friends while minimizing the amount of money that you spend when you are with them.

Hanging out with your friends should be fun, but not necessarily expensive. Take the initiative to suggest doing things that don't cost a lot of money.

Here are some suggestions:

-The Beach

-The Park

-Going for a walk

-A free or cheap concert if you can find one

-Working out together at the gym

There are plenty of things out there that can be a lot of fun if you just use your imagination. You have to embrace your surroundings and look at things from an optimistic point of view.

I remember going to a house party where everyone was hanging out in the basement. There was a pool table sitting right in the center of the basement, but nobody took the initiative to play.

A few hours had gone by before I asked one of my coworkers to play. I had to ask him 3 times before he finally agreed. It didn't take long before a ton of people started lining up next to us, so that they could play the winner.

Do you see how that works?

At first, nobody wanted to play pool because there wasn't anyone else playing. All it took was a couple of people to get things rolling, and then a lot of other people started joining in.

Originally, everyone was just standing around listening to loud music. I could have just left the pool table alone, but I chose to embrace my surroundings.

The things that you are doing don't have to cost a lot of money.

This might not work with everyone all the time, but generally, you just have to be able to show people that you're having a good time, and many of them will want to join you.

The activities that people choose to engage in are only as popular as what those very same people make them out to be.

If your friends are generally fun people, it shouldn't matter if what they are doing involves spending money or not. I think that we have allowed ourselves to become spoiled these days.

Many people just don't seem to be capable of using their imagination. I think that we can all learn a few things from some of the people that lived a century ago.

There are certain parks along with other places that regularly have "Live Music Festivals." Some places have bands performing either for free or for a small price.

You just have to put some effort into finding these places and events. I even remember going to an event where a lot of different bands actually played inside a restaurant. It turned out to be one of the best live performances I had ever been to.

Don't be afraid to break away from all of the hype. Don't automatically dismiss something just because it has a cheaper price tag on it.

Feeling like you have to spend money in order to have fun is not a good state of mind to be in.

Make it clear to your friends that you want to hang out with them, but you just don't have that much money to spend.

Just make sure that you're not always taking or borrowing money from them without ever giving anything back.

Hopefully, they will understand and respect your financial goals. Who knows? You might even motivate some of your friends to start doing the same thing.

Sometimes people just have to wait until they see the end result of what you are doing before they realize that they should have had more discipline themselves.

Meanwhile, just stay focused on the long-term.

Keep in mind that everything that you save money on now can add up and bring you something even better in the future.

Setting Financial Goals And Keeping Them In Front Of You

W hether or not you have anything specific that you would like to save your money for, it helps a lot to have a goal in front of you to focus on. You might have multiple goals that you would like to achieve in the future, but it's usually better to stay focused on one goal at a time.

Life will throw all sorts of distractions your way, and having an idea in your mind of what you would like to accomplish can help you to stay solid.

You don't even need to have a really specific type of goal in your mind, but you should at least have a general idea of what it is that you are saving your money for.

When I was saving my money for a car, I didn't know exactly what kind of car I was going to get; I just knew that I wanted a nice one that would also be reliable.

You will be less likely to waste your money on things that you don't need if you have a plan and a target to aim for. It can also be fun to think about the things that you can have after you have saved enough money for them.

I used to picture all of the benefits that I would have once I had my own car. I would picture what it would feel like to no longer have to stand at a bus stop for half an hour. I would think about how nice it would be to be able to drive my own car whenever I felt like driving it. It would also mean that I would no longer have to drive the same car that my parents would use.

Whatever it is that you would like your money to go to, picture all of the benefits that it offers.

Each time that you are tempted to spend your money on something that you don't really need, think about how nice it would be to save your money and accomplish your financial goal a day earlier.

If you don't have any goals right now, keep in mind that you probably will have some type of goals in the future, and when you do, it will be nice to have a head start on your savings plan.

Here are some examples of goals that you might wish to accomplish in the future:

-Getting a car

-Getting your own place

-Getting an air conditioner

-Getting a mini-fridge for your room

-Getting a new T.V.

-Going to school

The only things on this list that I had planned to get for months or years ahead of time were my car, and my air conditioner.

Everything else came in to the picture without much warning.

You can't always be sure of what you will encounter in the future, but it was nice to have the money there when I needed it for something.

There are so many things that could easily come up at the last minute.

Remember that there are things that can break that are going to need to be replaced. It can be difficult to keep track of everything, so it makes sense to plan ahead of time for the "unexpected."

These types of things don't have to be entirely unexpected if you are ready for them.

Saving Money On The Costs Of Your Car

Saving your money to buy a car is one thing, but the saving shouldn't stop after you make the purchase.

You not only want to save money on the car itself, but you want to save money on things such as maintenance as well.

When you look for cars to buy, you have some choices to consider.

An older car with high-mileage on it will usually be cheaper, but more likely to give you problems.

A brand new car will lose a lot of value almost as soon as you start driving it.

Many people that I've known seemed to like the idea of buying an old car with low miles.

They figured that the low-mileage was a good thing considering how long the car had been around. I decided that it made more sense to get a newer car with high-mileage on it.

If the car is only a couple of years old, but has 35,000 miles on it, that means that most of those miles are highway miles. I would rather have a newer car with the majority of the miles on it being highway miles than an old car that has been through a lot more stop and go city driving.

As long as the miles aren't too high on the newer car, it is usually a better choice than an old car with low-mileage or high-mileage.

The idea is to try to get the best of both worlds. You want a newer car without it being brand new. You also want it to have high-mileage, but not too high. You want the mileage to be high enough to know that most of the miles came from highway driving. You don't want the mileage to be high enough to create a lot of wear and tear on the car.

It's really a matter of personal preference when it comes to what type of car to get, but it makes sense to look for something that is fuel-efficient.

A sportier car with a bigger engine will usually make your insurance payments bigger.

Combine an older, sporty car with high-mileage on it, and you're probably asking for financial trouble.

Here are some tips to keep in mind when you're buying a car:

-Look for something that's fairly new, but not brand new

-Look for something with somewhat high-mileage, but not too high

-Look for something that is fuel-efficient

-Try not to get anything that is too sporty

-Don't just assume that an older car is in good shape just because it has low-mileage on it

When it's time to change the oil on your car, you can either do it yourself or pay someone to do it for you. I have to say that it really will not make or break your bank account either way.

You're really not saving that much money by changing the oil yourself, and you're not spending that much money on oil changes altogether.

If you do decide to start changing the oil yourself, you can save money each time by getting the cheaper oil and oil filters.

As long as you get the right weight and viscosity, it doesn't matter which brand you use, so it makes sense to go with the cheaper one.

For instance, your owner's manual might tell you to only use 5W-30. That means you cannot use 5W-20 or any other weight, but you can use whichever brand is the cheapest.

The same thing goes for the oil filter. Make sure that you get the right size for your car, but you can get whichever brand costs less money.

It's up to you to decide if it's worth it for you to change the oil yourself.

Keep in mind that you will also have to consider buying a couple of jacks and a jack stand if you wish to do it yourself. You will also be responsible for finding a place that accepts used motor oil after you're finished changing it.

Even with all the drawbacks that are involved in it, I have always liked to change the oil myself, but not to save money. I just like working on my own car, and I just happened to figure out how to do it while saving some money at the same time.

You can also save money by washing your own car. If you already have a hose, a sponge, and a bucket, the most expensive thing you should have to buy is a cloth that is specifically designed to absorb the water on the car. This will ensure that it doesn't leave too many marks on it from the water after you are finished.

Washing your car yourself can same you some money, but it will only add up in the long term. If you don't get your car washed that often to begin with, it's probably not worth it to wash it yourself.

The amount of money saved on car maintenance will also depend on where you choose to take your car, and what kind of deals the place you go to has going on.

Sometimes you can find coupons that offer a discount on the oil change when you take your car in to a certain shop. Sometimes automotive stores offer sales or special offers on certain brands of motor oil if you wish to do it yourself.

You will just have to do the math to decide which method will save you more money in the long term.

Saving Money While You Try Not To Starve

If you are at the point where your parents are starting to charge you money for food, or if you simply have to buy or chip in for your own food, then it's time to learn how to hold on to your body weight while trying not to lose too much of the weight that your wallet carries.

It helps to understand that fat will give you more calories per gram than carbohydrates or protein.

Obviously, you don't want to be eating only foods that are high in fat, or you will probably get sick.

You need a variety of things in your diet, but it does make sense to try to emphasize the things that give you the most calories for the least amount of money.

Since calories are used for energy, it makes sense to think of energy as something valuable.

Here is a pretty good list of healthy things that shouldn't set you back too far financially:

-Olive Oil

-Bagels

-Oatmeal

-Whole Milk

-Pasta

-Whole Wheat Bread

Oatmeal, bread, and pasta can make you feel fuller than many other types of food, even though they are not particularly high in calories. This can help you save money by consuming less food without losing energy.

You will probably also want to include meat, and some organic fruits and vegetables. Those will not be cheap, but having even a small supply of them around is better than nothing.

Personally, I know that I start to feel like I have less energy when I go longer than a couple of days without having at least a small portion of chicken or beef.

When you add up the amount of calories that something like oatmeal and whole milk provide, you will realize that you are getting a better deal than you would for most other things.

You can add olive oil to your bread or pasta for some extra calories.

With the exception of organic fruits and vegetables, you should try to put your grocery money towards the things that offer more calories.

Everyone has a certain amount of calories that they need to consume daily.

The amount of calories that you need will depend on how active you are.

When you go out to eat, look for things that are actually worth getting.

It doesn't make any sense to spend $10 on a salad with bread and soup on the side.

You could make yourself something more filling at home for a lot cheaper.

Consider which items on the menu will offer you the most high quality calories for the least amount of money.

Don't spend your money on things that offer you less value than what you already have inside your kitchen.

Maximizing Your Wallet With A Minimalist Attitude

Y ou don't have to become a true minimalist in order to save some extra money, but it can help to take the time to seriously consider all of the things that you don't really need in your life.

You really can't assume that having more expensive things in your life will automatically make you a happier person.

I actually noticed myself becoming more stressed out as I began to accumulate more and more expensive things.

Cars develop problems, expensive items get stolen, and there is always the possibility of your stuff being destroyed in a fire or a flood.

It's a lot easier to appreciate the things that you have when you have less of them. We start to forget the meaning of thankfulness as all of the things that we own begin to pile up.

People start to obsess about their cars, hoping that they don't get stolen or broken into. They spend a ton of money on insurance in order to protect themselves from anything that might happen. They basically spend money to protect themselves from losing more money on the thing that they spent money on.

It just never seems to end.

Cars are just an example. Some people need cars, and some people don't. You will have to be really honest with yourself as you decide which things you need, and which things you don't need. You might be surprised with how little you actually need.

You don't have to do anything extreme right away, but you should make an effort to focus only on the most important things that you can't live without. It's alright to to reward yourself by spending money on something that you want, but make sure that you set boundaries for yourself.

Don't spend enough money to make yourself regret your purchase later on, and certainly don't invest more money in something than you can afford to lose.

When you are really tempted to spend a lot of money on something that you don't need, remind yourself of all the bad things that will come along with it.

A brand new video game console can be a distraction when you could be doing more productive things. A car means less exercise from walking, and more bills to pay.

Don't be afraid of spending any of your money, but make sure that you are aware of the impact that your purchases will have.

Think about your future and use your best judgment to make the right choices.

Don't Get Carried Away With Your Credit Card

C redit cards can come in handy, but you should not use them unless you are absolutely certain that you will be able to pay off your bill right away.

Don't carry balances by only paying the minimum amount due, and then paying off the rest later. Just because carrying balances is an option, that doesn't mean that it's a good option for you.

Make sure that you are able to completely pay off the whole thing right away.

You don't want to mess up your credit rating, especially at such a young age. Give the credit card to your parents if you have to, and let them help you monitor yourself.

Sometimes it helps to get another opinion, and your parents can let you know if they think that you are using your credit card too often.

Don't just assume that you will have the money in your bank account by the time your credit card bill arrives.

Make sure that you have more than enough money in your account to cover the bill from the minute you use the credit card to the day that you receive your statement.

Don't forget that you can't let your bank balance fall below a certain amount of money. Let's say that you have a $200 credit card bill to pay off with only $300 in your bank account. You will get a penalty if your bank account is not supposed to fall below $200 and you let it fall down to $100.

Be responsible with your credit card. After all, if you can't even be responsible with a credit card, how are you going to handle the bigger things in life?

Saving Money, And Thinking About The Future

There is always the possibility that you might change your mind about certain things in the future.

Things change, people change, and plans change. You might still live at home, or you might move out.

You might end up buying an expensive house, or you might end up getting a good deal on a small condo. You might be able to get around without a car for now, but you might end up needing one in another 5 years.

We have our goals for the future, but we can't always predict the obstacles that we will have to face. It's good to live in the present moment, but we need to think about the future when it comes to how we choose to spend our money.

Don't think that 10 years is too far away when you think about saving money.

If it takes you years and years to save enough money for something that's really important, 10 years might not be so far away after all. I used to think things like, "So what? That's years away." I could have saved so much more money if I just had the right kind of motivation.

You can't always assume that you will just fall into a ton of money in the future somehow. You can start making things happen now by saving money as you think about your future. Give yourself a break later on by saving money now.

Don't be too hard on yourself, but don't go so easy on yourself either.

It's alright to occasionally spend more money than you would have liked.

Don't drive yourself crazy by never allowing yourself to buy something that you want.

Saving money not only requires time, but practice.

As you practice thinking about all of the money that you will need in the future, you will slip deeper into the habit of saving your money in the present.

How to Fix Your Credit
How to Raise Your Credit Score
By David A. Hunter

Table of Contents

Intro

Having good credit is necessary for many things in life, such as:

- **Taking out a mortgage on a house**
- **Taking out a car loan**
- **Paying lower premiums to insurance companies**
- **Getting a cellphone contract**
- **Renting an apartment**

Even certain employers might run credit reports on potential prospects as part of the background check during the interviewing process.

Maintaining a good credit score can help you save money by keeping you qualified for credit cards and loans at the most favorable terms.

Unfortunately, there are some drawbacks that go along with the benefit of being able to borrow money.

One of the drawbacks is the potential for identity theft.

People can steal your personal information and use it to take out credit in your name, damaging your credit score in the process.

Identity theft is very common and seems to be increasing in recent years.

Errors on your credit report can certainly be frustrating, especially if you don't know how to correct them.

Generally, credit scores are determined by:

- **payment history on credit cards and loans**
- **length of time you've had accounts open**
- **frequency in which you apply for new credit**

• **how much credit you use on a regular basis**

But sometimes things happen that are out of our control. You might be interested in disputing something on your credit report, but are unsure of how to do so.

Perhaps your credit score has been damaged, and now you would like to fix it. Or maybe you have no credit at all, and you would like to learn how to build it for the first time.

Either way, this book is intended to help you.

It will cover:

• **How to build credit when you don't have any**

• **How credit scores are calculated**

• **How to dispute errors on your credit report**

• **Where to Go for Credit Assistance**

How to Build Credit When You Don't Have Any

Building credit for the first time can be tricky. When you have no credit history currently established, many lenders will refuse to loan you money.

Credit history is generally established by:

- **Having your own credit card and using it regularly**
- **Making regular payments on a loan**
- **Making monthly payments on a mortgage**

It seems confusing and even frustrating because in most cases, you need to already have credit in order to obtain credit.

If you apply for your first credit card in order to build credit, you may be rejected for having no previous credit history.

So how is a person supposed to get credit in the first place?

Thankfully, there are indeed some ways to build credit from the ground up.

Credit Cards

Although it might feel like searching for a needle in a haystack, there are credit cards out there that can be used by people with no credit history.

These are referred to as *secured credit cards*.

They work by putting a certain amount of money (usually a few hundred to several hundred dollars) into the credit card account as collateral.

So just in case you miss a payment, the credit card company will simply take the money out of your account to cover the costs.

For example, if you apply for a secured credit card, the company might require you to put five-hundred dollars into an account. If you have a $250 bill that you do not pay on time, your account will cover you.

Of course, that's not a good reason to not pay a bill on time. Even if there is sufficient money in your account to cover the bills, missing a payment can still have a negative impact on your credit score.

Try to get something with a VISA logo on it, as this is what seems to be most commonly accepted by businesses when it comes to credit cards. MASTERCARD would be a good second choice.

A potential drawback is that secured credit cards usually don't come with much purchasing power, so you might eventually get frustrated with the lack of spending freedom.

Another drawback is that these types of credit cards might come with an annual fee, as well as other fees.

For these reasons, you might want to use it as a stepping stone for another credit card.

You can use a card like this to build credit for 6 to 12 months (or however long it takes), and then get an upgraded credit card. When you choose to close your account, your security deposit will be refunded to you.

Keep in mind that spending more money will not help you build credit faster. It's more about using the credit card regularly (on a monthly basis), and paying the bills on time.

Don't carry balances.

When the credit card statement tells you to pay the *minimum balance* by a certain date, try to pay the full balance each time to avoid paying interest fees.

Since lenders take more multiple things into consideration when deciding whether or not they should qualify you, simply being able to put money into an account for collateral might not be enough of a reason for them to grant you a credit card. They take other things into consideration, such as, income, expenditures, and employment history.

Here are some secured credit cards that can be applied for:

Note: Always verify the terms with the company before applying.

Open Sky Credit Card

CITI Secured MASTERCARD

Capital One Secured MASTERCARD

Armed Forces Bank VISA

PRIMOR VISA

Navy Federal Credit Union VISA

Auto Loans

Taking out an auto loan when you have little to no credit history will typically require a cosigner. Getting a parent to cosign with you on an auto loan will split the responsibility between the two of you, therefore, sharing the burden if you miss a payment, and sharing the benefit of credit building if you make your payments on time.

Since it's a loan that drags on for months or years at a time, you will have to pay interest, so you might not want to wait very long before paying the vehicle off.

For instance, if you are paying five-hundred dollars a year in interest, instead of taking taking five years to pay off the loan, try to get it paid off in two or three years.

The strategy here is to find a happy middle ground that is best for you. Five years of making payments on time is good for credit building, but doing the same thing in two years will save you money on interest.

* * *

When you are starting out, paying your bills on time is critical. Be careful not to spend more than you can afford to pay back.

Instead of focusing on building credit, it might help to focus more on not ruining your credit. If you focus too much on building credit, you might be tempted to use your credit card more often than you can afford to.

Remember, it's not about how much money you spend.

Even if you are only putting ten dollars a month on your credit card, you will still be building credit as long as you consistently pay it off on time.

How Credit Scores are Calculated

If you have ever looked up your credit score, you may have wondered why each major credit bureau showed a different number.

The three major credit bureaus (Experian, Equifax, and TransUnion) all have different credit scoring models.

In addition to the three major credit bureaus using different methods to calculate credit scores, different lenders and creditors may choose to report to different bureaus.

A certain credit card company might only report to Equifax, while a particular lender might report to TransUnion and Experian. Another lender might not report report to any of the bureaus at all.

Since none of these credit bureaus are part of the United States government, reporting to them is optional.

Creditors and lenders can *choose* to report to them, but it is not required.

Payment history doesn't go straight to the credit bureaus by default; it goes to the creditors and lenders, and it will only reach the bureaus if they decide to report it to them.

Different companies might prioritize certain things over others.

For instance, an auto lender might emphasize a person's payment history, while a mortgage company might place more emphasis on the person's employment history. Other lenders might take a more balanced approach and look carefully at multiple things, prioritizing them equally.

The criteria they have to choose from to calculate your credit score include:

- **Payment history**
- **Number of inquiries the person has**
- **How old the accounts are**

- **Amount of debt the person has**

Payment history and amount of debt the person has are two of the largest contributing factors to a person's credit score.

Having a too many high-balance accounts or maxed-out credit cards could negatively impact a credit score.

As for percentage, the breakdown for FICO credit calculation can be found on their website, which states that they use :

- 35% payment history
- 30% amounts owed
- 15% length of credit history
- 10% new credit
- 10% credit mix

Note: Closed accounts, and the credit history that is related to them, will still influence a person's FICO scores.

Since credit mix is only ten percent of what FICO uses to calculate a credit score, it doesn't make much sense to apply for a significant number of new credit cards to try speeding up the process of building or repairing credit. This is particularly true if you do not have a long credit history.

New accounts can lower the average account age, and if you do not have enough alternative credit information to work with, it can have a larger effect on your FICO score.

If there are any questions about rules or legalities, you might benefit from reading the Fair Credit Reporting Act (FCRA).

How to Dispute Errors on Your Credit Report

I t is recommended that you review your credit report on a regular basis to ensure that there are no errors on it.

It is particularly beneficial to check your credit report before applying for a loan, buying insurance, or even applying for a job, so that you're not setting yourself up for rejection.

Errors on credit reports are often caused by fraudulent activity due to identity theft. Delinquency can result when someone uses your information to open an account in your name and not pay the bills.

Whether you are dealing with erroneous inquiries or medical collections, the process for getting it straightened out is generally the same.

A credit inquiry is when a financial institution makes a request for credit report information from a credit reporting agency.

There are two types of credit inquiries:

1.) **Hard inquiry**- usually happens when a financial institution checks a person's credit when that person initiates it. For example, if you apply for a credit card, that means *you* initiated the situation. Hard inquiries typically lower a person's credit score, but not significantly, unless perhaps the person has many hard inquiries within a relatively short time.

2.) **Soft inquiry**- usually happens when someone else initiates the situation. For example, a credit card company wants to reach out to you about an offer they have, so they run a background check to see how you might qualify, before sending you an advertisement in the mail. Soft inquiries do not have an effect on credit scores, although they might go on record in credit reports.

Before you even attempt to remove inquiries, it's important to make sure that you did not authorize them. If you authorized them, it is highly unlikely you will be able to remove them before they finish running their course.

In most cases, a hard inquiry will affect a person's credit score for a year, although it can remain on the credit report for two years, assuming it was authorized by the person whose credit score was affected by it.

Certain inquiries might be eligible for deletion, while others might not be.

If you're not the one who applied for a new account or new form of credit, you can request a removal of the hard inquiry.

When looking over your credit report, you might find an inquiry from an organization that is not familiar to you.

Before trying to remove the inquiries, try to clear up any misunderstanding that might have occurred.

Since companies sometimes change names or get bought out by other companies, make sure the unfamiliar-sounding company is not actually a company that you transacted business with in the past.

Other times, a lender might actually submit an application to multiple organizations to see if they can find you a better deal. That can lead to more than one inquiry.

Equifax, Experian, and TransUnion are required to provide a free annual credit report to you, but you will have to request it. Once requested and received, you will not be able to check the report again for free for another twelve months.

If you do happen to have errors on your credit report, there are some steps you can take to dispute them, but many people seem to do it incorrectly.

- **Order your credit report by mail**

- **Dispute the error(s) with the credit bureau**

- **Dispute the errors with the organization that forwards your information to the credit reporting company**

- **Get the debt validated (if necessary)**

Ordering your credit report

To begin the process of correcting errors on your credit report, you should order your credit report by mail.

Although you can order your free annual credit report online, if you already know there are errors on your report, it is better to order it offline.

Ordering the credit report will allow you to have a reference to work with while disputing the errors that you have found.

Additionally, ordering offline specifically makes it easier to attach any necessary documentation to help support your case. It also allows written results to be mailed to you.

Note: the annualcreditreport.com website applies mainly to credit cards. If you are looking for mortgage approval, you might see a different score than the score your mortgage lender will see when he or she uses a different source to run a credit report on you.

To order your credit report, request it by filling out a credit report request form. A link is provided below, but you can also simply perform an online search for, "annual credit report request form," and go from there.

After completing the Annual Credit Report Request Form, mail it to:

Annual Credit Report Request Service

P.O. Box 105281

Atlanta, GA 30348-5281

Your request should be processed withing a period of fifteen days.

Disputing the errors with the credit bureau

The next step is to dispute the error(s) with the credit reporting company. Notify them about which part of the credit report is inaccurate, sending documentation to help back up your statement.

When sending in documents to support your case, make copies to send out, so you can keep the originals for your own records.

Make sure the letter that you send clearly identifies the items you are disputing.

You can help clarify by highlighting or circling the parts of the text on the credit report where the errors appear. But use a copy of the report to send to them, and keep the original one for your own records.

Don't forget to mention why you are disputing the information. The more clarity you provide, the better.

Only send your dispute letter to the credit bureau that has been recorded with. For example, if the errors are only showing up on the TransUnion credit report, don't send a dispute letter to Experian or Equifax.

To dispute an error on your credit report with an individual credit bureau, visit the following websites to fill out and print their forms, and then mail them to the appropriate addresses:

Submit dispute to TransUnion

https://www.transunion.com/docs/rev/personal/InvestigationRequest.pdf

TransUnion Consumer Solutions

P.O. Box 2000

Chester, PA 19022-2000

Submit dispute to Equifax

https://www.equifax.com/cp/MailInDislcosureRequest.pdf

Equifax Information Services LLC

P.O. Box 740256

Atlanta, GA 30348

Submit dispute to Experian

https://www.experian.com/assets/rentbureau/general/dispute_form.pdf

P.O. Box 26

Credit companies have to at least consider investigating your dispute because that's the law. The process should be complete within 30 days, but try to allow a little extra time for the mail to reach your address.

Upon completion of the investigation, the credit reporting company has to send you the outcome in writing.

Disputing the errors with the organization that forwards your information to the credit reporting company

The company or organization that forwards information about you to the credit bureau can be a credit card company, cell phone company, mortgage lender, etc.

Similar to the last step, dispute the item(s) in writing, adding along any documentation (copies, not originals) that could help prove your case.

As for where to send the letter and documentation, simply use the address provided on the address of your credit report. But if no address is provided, contact the company to ask where you should send the letter. As a final option, you can send the letter to any business address for that company, and hopefully, they will take care of it.

As long as the organization continues to report the disputed item to a credit bureau, it is required to also notify them that the item has indeed been disputed.

If the disputed items are determined to be accurate, the organization is required to notify the credit bureau to have the disputed items updated or deleted.

As far as what to say in the dispute letters, I think a lot of people might be making the process more complicated than it has to be. Simply inform them of the inaccurate information, why you believe it is inaccurate, and request that the errors be removed. Tell them you have circled or highlighted the items that are erroneous, and provide them with the name of the company that has reported the inaccurate information.

Even though it costs extra money, try to send the letters by certified mail, so there will be proof that the intended recipients received them since someone has to sign for it.

Debt Validation

Hopefully, the previous steps will have solved the problem. But just in case a company employee does not agree with you and chooses to keep the errors on your report, there is an additional step you can take.

You have a legal right to obtain verification of the debt.

This will create more work for them because they have to send proof of the debt to confirm that it is genuine.

A debt collection agency is an organization that pursues debts on the creditor's behalf.

The debt collector might call you on the phone. But the phone call should be followed up with a written response from them.

After initial communication with you, the debt collector is required to send a written notice of debt validation to you within 5 days. You will then have the right to dispute the validity of the debt within a 30 day time frame.

If you don't get the debt validation letter within 5 days, call the debt collector and request it. Verify your preferred address, so they can send it to the correct place.

The notice they send you should include information such as:

• Creditor's name

• Amount to be collected

• That you can request to have the original creditor's identify revealed to you in writing within a 30 day time period if it happens to be different from the current creditor, just in case there was any misunderstanding.

As with the previous steps, make the request in writing, preferably through certified mail with a return receipt requested.

Try not to make things more complicated than they have to be. In the letter that you send to them, simply mention that you are responding to the notice you received for the debt being claimed against you.

Mention your name and the date you received the notice. Tell them you are requesting verification of the debt, including the age of the debt, the name and address of the original creditor, an itemized statement of what is owed, and evidence that you are legally responsible for the debt.

Tell them that if there is no evidence of this debt found in your name, you request that the credit bureaus and any financial institutions involved be notified about it, so the issue can be rectified.

Toward the end of the letter, provide your preferred address and tell them to communicate with you by mail.

Be polite and professional.

After you've sent the validation request, there is no clear deadline for when the collector has to respond.

Generally, the more proof you send them to back up your case about the debt not belonging to you, the easier you will make it for them to agree with you.

Where to Go for Credit Assistance

W hen you need assistance with getting issues related to your credit straightened out, there are some options available.

Identity Theft

If your particular case is fraud-related, there are some organizations you can reach out to, including:

- https://www.identitytheft.gov/
- Internet Crime Complaint Center
- https://www.fraud.org/
- Identity Theft Resource Center
- Contact the credit bureaus and have them place a credit freeze or fraud alert on your credit report. A three-month fraud alert is fairly simple to have done, but a seven-year fraud alert requires that you file a police report in relation to the identity theft that occurred.

Credit Counseling

Credit counseling is typically free and available to consumers that would like assistance in getting out of debt. The financial counseling agencies can give you a suggested budget to work with and a creditor review.

Credit counseling agencies can work with low-income individuals and individuals who can't afford to pay.

Credit councilors can be found at:

- https://www.nfcc.org/ (800) 388-2227
- https://fcaa.org/ (800) 450-1794

- https://www.militaryonesource.mil/ (800) 342-9647 (this option is for military members)

Credit Repair Companies

If you feel like you have exhausted your free options and are still struggling to repair your credit, credit repair companies offer to improve your credit for a fee.

But it is very important to verify the legitimacy of these companies before doing business with them.

Other

- https://careconnectusa.org/

Offers help with collections, student loan relief, child care assistance, debt relief, free bankruptcy advice, and more.

- https://www.consumerfinance.gov/

Offers answers to hundreds of financial questions.

<u>Closing</u>

Building and repairing credit can take quite a while, but trying to take shortcuts will oftentimes lead to more frustration.

Try to practice being patient as you wait for the results.

If you feel stressed out during the process, give yourself enough time to engage in other activities. Pet a dog, take a walk, and try to give yourself a break.

It can also help to change your perspective. Even though establishing a good credit history can be important, credit scores are still essentially just numbers on a screen, so try to look at it that way. Credit isn't everything.

Stay calm, be happy, and be persistent with building and repairing your credit.

www.ingramcontent.com/pod-product-compliance
Lightning Source LLC
Chambersburg PA
CBHW030735180526
45157CB00008BA/3178